TIME TELLING
INTRODUCING QUARTERS AND FIVE MINUTES
PRACTICE WORKSHEETS

WORKBOOK WITH ANSWERS

A Complete Guide to Learning Basic Time Telling to the Quarter Hour and Five Minutes Using Various Easy to Grasp Exercises

By Shobha

VOLUME I

Table of Contents

Analog Clock Reference

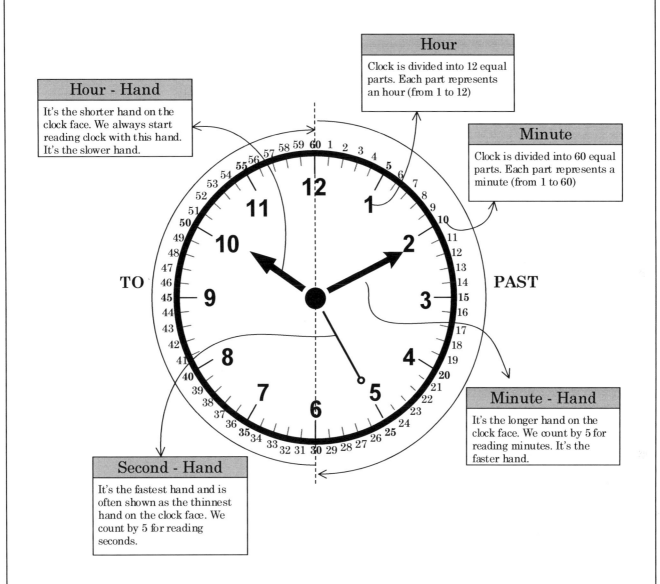

Hour - Hand
It's the shorter hand on the clock face. We always start reading clock with this hand. It's the slower hand.

Hour
Clock is divided into 12 equal parts. Each part represents an hour (from 1 to 12)

Minute
Clock is divided into 60 equal parts. Each part represents a minute (from 1 to 60)

Minute - Hand
It's the longer hand on the clock face. We count by 5 for reading minutes. It's the faster hand.

Second - Hand
It's the fastest hand and is often shown as the thinnest hand on the clock face. We count by 5 for reading seconds.

TO   PAST

In a day there are 24 hours so the hour hand has to make two complete revolutions every day.

In an hour there are 60 minutes so the minute hand has to make one complete revolution every hour. So if the hour hand traverses from 12 to 1 then the minute hand would move 60 places making one complete revolution of the clock.

In a minute there are 60 seconds so the second hand has to make one complete revolution every minute. So if the minute hand traverses from 1 to 2 (see smaller numbers on outer periphery of the clock above) then the second hand would move 60 places making one complete revolution of the clock.

Before we start practicing and acquiring this important time telling skill, we must understand that it's very simple and fun to learn time telling and it can easily be achieved with regular consistent practice. If you have a digital clock at home then even though it would be painful, try to avoid seeing time in it for some time until you are comfortable telling time with an analog clock.

Before You Start Telling The Time

Before learning to tell time it's recommended to learn the skills listed below:
- Counting up to 60
- Skip counting by 5s (5 times table) → Being able to quickly tell 5, 10, 15, 20, etc. helps understand the movement of the minute hand on a clock.
- Distinguish clock hands by their length

How To Tell Time

Closely look at the clock on the previous page. See how numbers to represent hours (big numbers) and minutes (small numbers) are laid on the clock face. Observe that each position on the clock face has two different numbers assigned to it – the big number and the small number. Big numbers are always used for telling hours and small numbers are used for telling minutes. In regular clocks smaller numbers are not marked. So how would you find minutes? Don't worry! It's very easy. You just need to count by 5s to get minutes. If you have already learnt basic multiplication, then you just multiply the big number by 5 to get the minutes. Look at the pattern below. This helps understand how minutes are progressing with each number that represents an hour.

Hour	1	2	3	4	5	6	7	8	9	10	11	12
Minute	*5*	*10*	*15*	*20*	*25*	*30*	*35*	*40*	*45*	*50*	*55*	*60*

Also remember the following

☞ **Hour Hand is shorter and mostly thicker**

☞ **Minute Hand is longer and mostly thinner**

☞ **When the minute hand is pointing at 12, it's the exact hour and no minutes have passed**

Now let's look at a step by step method to tell time

STEP – 1

Look at the clock on the right. Now find the position of the hour hand.

In this case it's between Four and Five.

Take the lower of the two numbers which is **Four**.
This tells us the hour of the day.

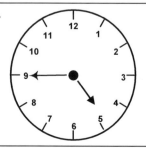

STEP – 2

Look at the clock on the right. Now find the number that the minute hand is pointing at.

In this case it's at **Nine.**

This tells us the minute of the hour.

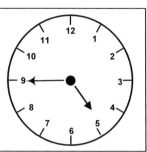

STEP – 3

Count by 5s nine times. 5, 10, 15, 20, 25, 30, 35, 40, **45.**

If you know multiplication, then directly get the minutes by multiplying 9 and 5. i.e. 9 x 5 = 45.

So the minute of the hour is **45**. We also call it "**quarter-to**" the next hour or "**quarter-till**" to the next hour.

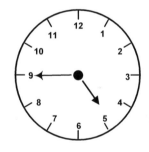

STEP – 4

Put all the information together.

→ The Hour is Four
→ The Minute is 45

So the time of the day is Forty Five Past Four.
In the next quarter hour, it is going to be Five O'Clock so we can also call it "Quarter to Five".
In digital format it can be written as 4:45.

Elapsed Time

Now that we have learnt how to tell time let's take a look at elapsed time. Elapsed time is the amount of time that has passed between two events. When you hear something like "time spent", "how long", "time passed", "time difference", etc. that basically means we are talking about elapsed time. Look at the below clocks and try to find elapsed time between them.

START TIME

END TIME

First clock shows 1:35 and the second clock shows 2:10.

START TIME = Twenty-Five to Two
END TIME = Ten past Two

So the elapsed time = 35 minutes.

Elapsed Time Using The Number Line

Did you know we can also represent a clock on a number line as shown below?

Now let's solve an elapsed time problem using the above number line.

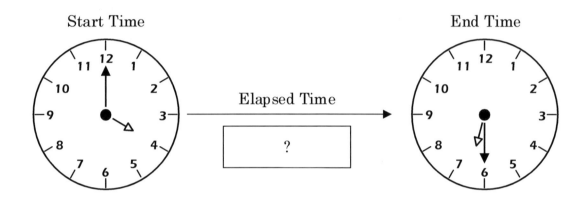

Mark the start time and end time on the number line and then see how many hops you would make from the start time mark to reach the end time mark.

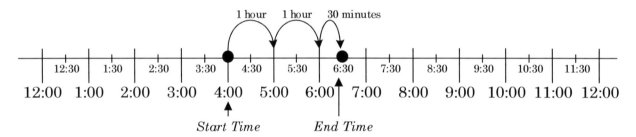

From the clocks shown above, we marked the start time at 4:00 and the end time at 6:30 on the number line.

Now let's start hopping forward starting from the 4:00 mark one step at a time.

After the first hop we are at 5:00. We are still behind the 6:30 mark. So let's make another hop to reach the 6:00 mark. Keep counting how many hops you are making as that would give us the number of hours elapsed. So after the second hop we are at 6:00 but still behind the 6:30 mark. However, this time we do not need to make another full hop as that would take us to 7:00 which is after the 6:30 mark. So make a half hop to land on 6:30.

Now let's look at the number of hops we made so far. We made two full hops from the 4:00 mark to the 5:00 mark and then from the 5:00 mark to the 6:00 mark. We also made a half hop from the 6:00 mark to the 6:30 mark. So the total elapsed time is 2 hours and 30 minutes.

Date: _____   Start: _____   Finish: _____   Score: _____

What time does the clock show? Fill the box. Example: Quarter Past Four.

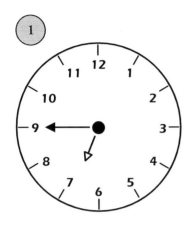

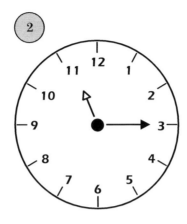

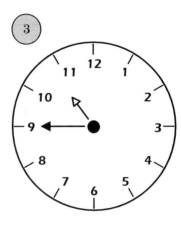

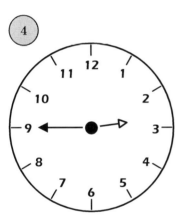

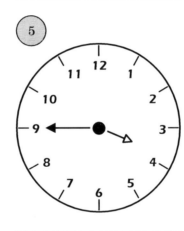

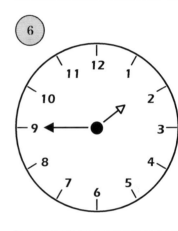

Date: _____ Start: _____ Finish: _____ Score: _____

What time does the clock show? Fill the box. Example: Quarter Past Four.

1

2

3

[ ]

[ ]

[ ]

4

5

6

[ ]

[ ]

[ ]

7

8

9

[ ]

[ ]

[ ]

Date: _____ Start: _____ Finish: _____ Score: _____

What time does the clock show? Fill the box. Example: Quarter Past Four.

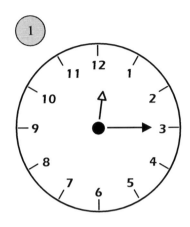

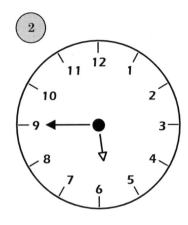

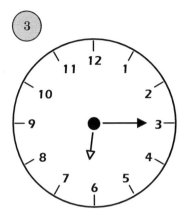

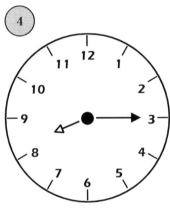

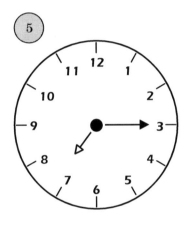

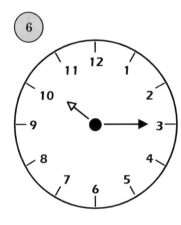

Date: _____   Start: _____   Finish: _____   Score: _____

What time does the clock show? Fill the box. Example: Quarter Past Four.

① [clock]

[   ]

② [clock]

[   ]

③ [clock]

[   ]

④ [clock]

[   ]

⑤ [clock]

[   ]

⑥ [clock]

[   ]

⑦ [clock]

[   ]

⑧ [clock]

[   ]

⑨ [clock]

[   ]

Date: _____ Start: _____ Finish: _____ Score: _____

What time does the clock show? Fill the box. Example: Quarter Past Four.

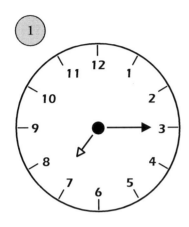 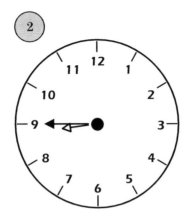 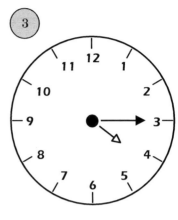

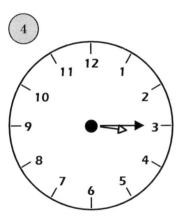 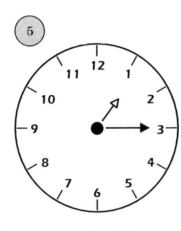 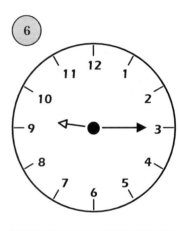

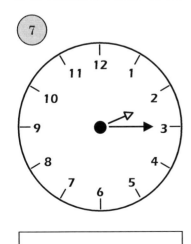 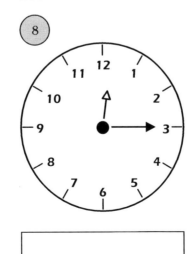

Date:_____   Start:_____   Finish:_____   Score:_____

What time does the clock show? Fill the box. Example: Quarter Past Four.

1

2

3

4

5

6

7

8

9

Date: _____ Start: _____ Finish: _____ Score: _____

Draw the hands to show the time.

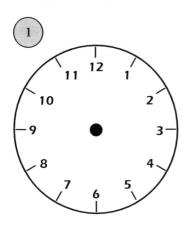

Quarter past four

Quarter to twelve

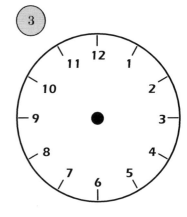

Quarter past three

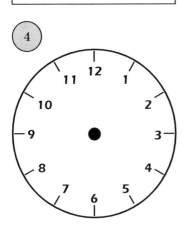

Quarter past eight

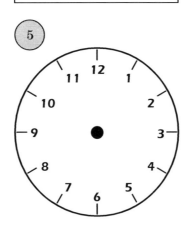

Quarter past five

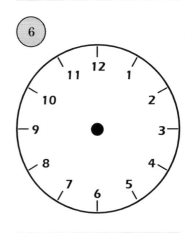

Quarter past six

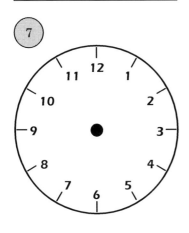

Quarter past nine

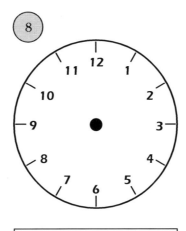

Quarter past twelve

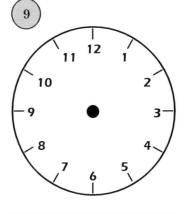

Quarter past one

Date: _____ Start: _____ Finish: _____ Score: _____

Draw the hands to show the time.

①

Quarter to five

②

Quarter past seven

③

Quarter to twelve

④

Quarter to seven

⑤

Quarter to ten

⑥

Quarter to nine

⑦

Quarter to thirteen

⑧

Quarter to two

⑨

Quarter to four

Date: _____   Start: _____   Finish: _____   Score: _____

Draw the hands to show the time.

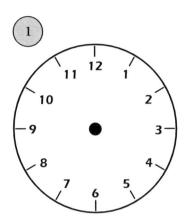

1

Quarter past nine

2

Quarter to six

3

Quarter past one

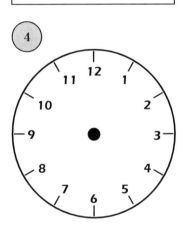

4

Quarter past seven

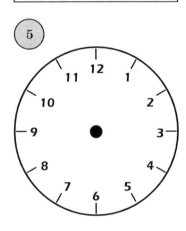

5

Quarter past ten

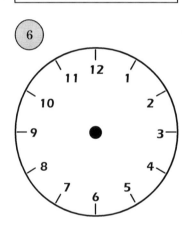

6

Quarter past three

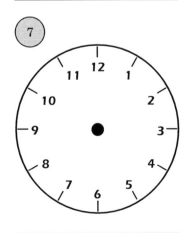

7

Quarter past two

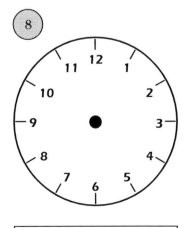

8

Quarter past twelve

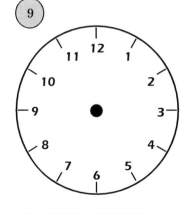

9

Quarter past eight

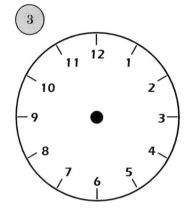

Date: _____ Start: _____ Finish: _____ Score: _____

Draw the hands to show the time.

①

Quarter to two

②

Quarter past twelve

③

Quarter to five

④

Quarter to eleven

⑤

Quarter to six

⑥

Quarter to nine

⑦

Quarter to eight

⑧

Quarter to ten

⑨

Quarter to three

Date: _____   Start: _____   Finish: _____   Score: _____

Draw the hands to show the time.

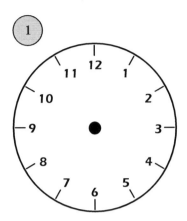

Quarter past three

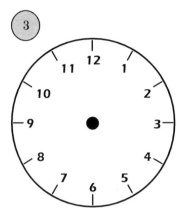

Quarter to five

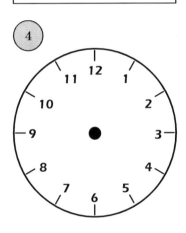

Quarter past twelve

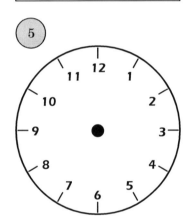

Quarter past ten

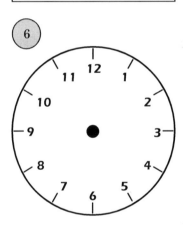

Quarter past seven

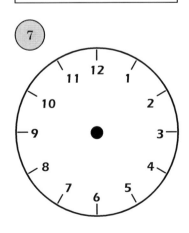

Quarter past six

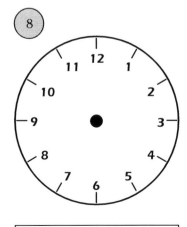

Quarter past eight

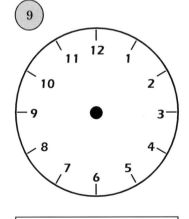

Quarter past two

Quarter past nine

Date: _____ Start: _____ Finish: _____ Score: _____

Draw the hands to show the time.

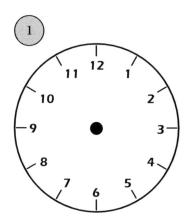

Quarter past eight

Quarter to four

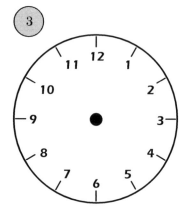

Quarter past five

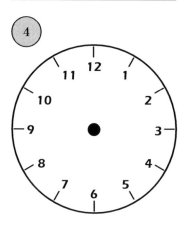

Quarter past six

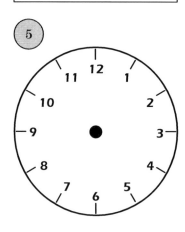

Quarter past two

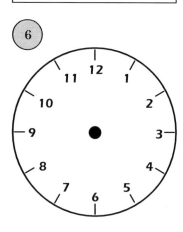

Quarter past one

Quarter past seven

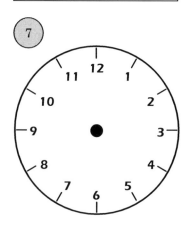

Quarter past eleven

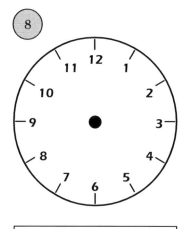

Quarter past four

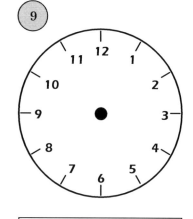

Date: _____ Start: _____ Finish: _____ Score: _____

What time does the clock show? Write in the box. Example: 2:15.

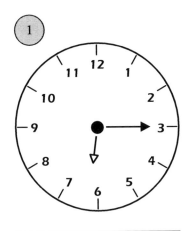

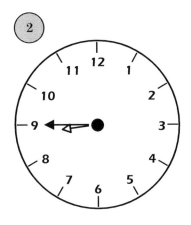

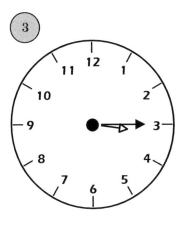

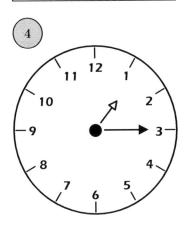

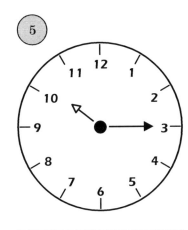

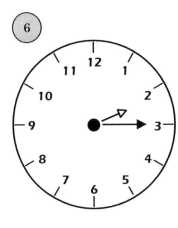

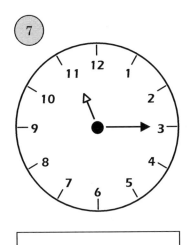

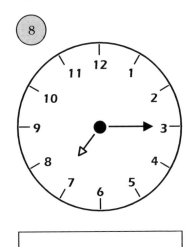

Date: _____ Start: _____ Finish: _____ Score: _____

What time does the clock show? Write in the box. Example: 2:15.

1

2

3

4

5

6

7

8

9

Time Telling – Introducing Quarters and Five Minutes

Date:_____ Start:_____ Finish:_____ Score:_____

What time does the clock show? Write in the box. Example: 2:15.

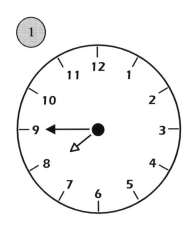

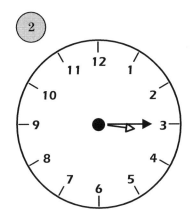

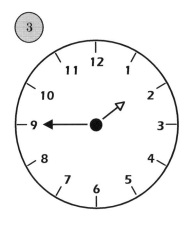

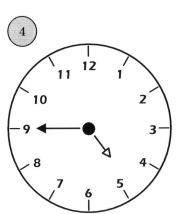

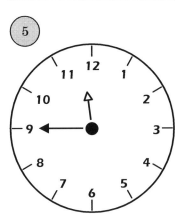

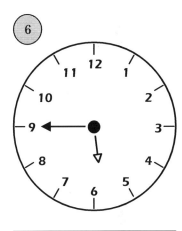

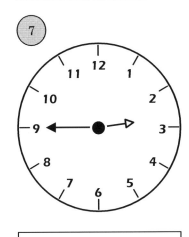

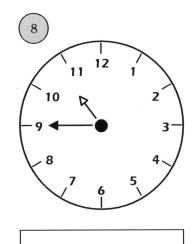

Time Telling – Introducing Quarters and Five Minutes

Date: _____ Start: _____ Finish: _____ Score: _____

What time does the clock show? Write in the box. Example: 2:15.

①

②

③

④

⑤

⑥

⑦

⑧

⑨

Date: _____   Start: _____   Finish: _____   Score: _____

What time does the clock show? Write in the box. Example: 2:15.

1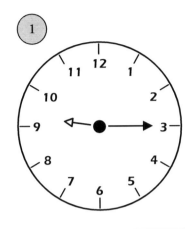

2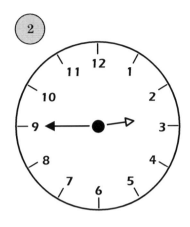

3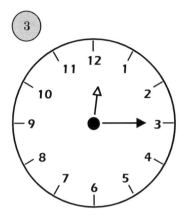

4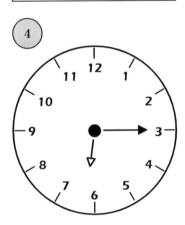

5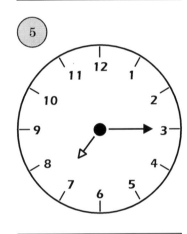

6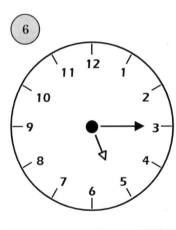

7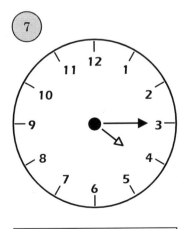

8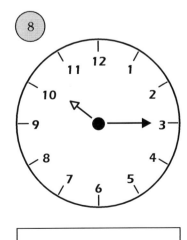

9

Date: _____ Start: _____ Finish: _____ Score: _____

What time does the clock show? Write in the box. Example: 2:15.

1

2

3

4

5

6

7

8

9

Date:_____   Start:_____   Finish:_____   Score:_____

Draw the hands to show the time.

①
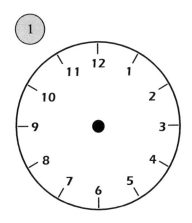

| 12:45 |

②

| 7:15 |

③
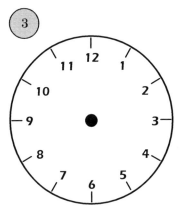

| 10:45 |

④

| 5:45 |

⑤

| 4:45 |

⑥
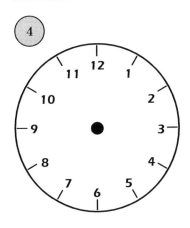

| 8:45 |

⑦
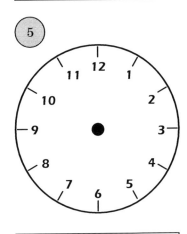

| 11:45 |

⑧
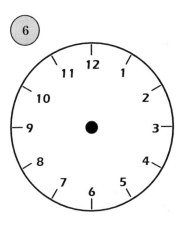

| 1:45 |

⑨
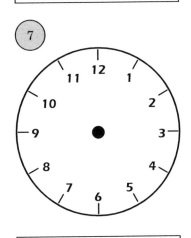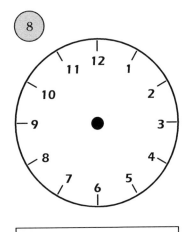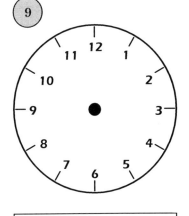

| 6:45 |

Date: _____ Start: _____ Finish: _____ Score: _____

Draw the hands to show the time.

①

3:15

②

7:45

③

2:15

④

10:15

⑤

5:15

⑥

9:15

⑦

6:15

⑧

1:15

⑨

11:15

Date: _____ Start: _____ Finish: _____ Score: _____

Draw the hands to show the time.

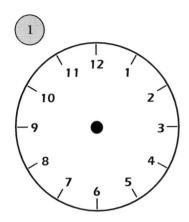

6:45

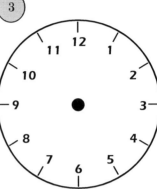

7:15

3:45

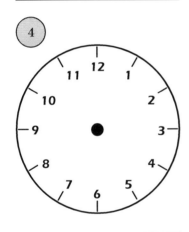

9:45

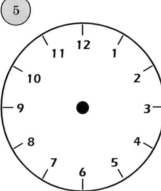

4:45

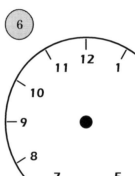

1:45

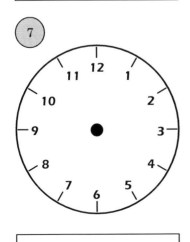

10:45

5:45

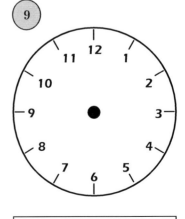

8:45

Date: _____   Start: _____   Finish: _____   Score: _____

Draw the hands to show the time.

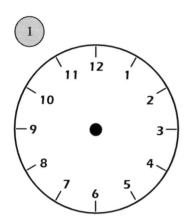

| 2:45 |

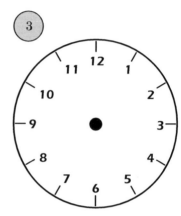

| 8:15 |

| 6:45 |

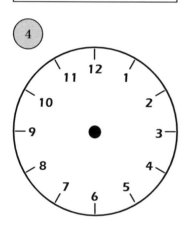

| 3:45 |

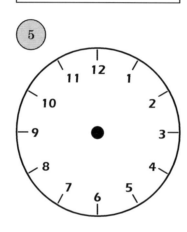

| 11:45 |

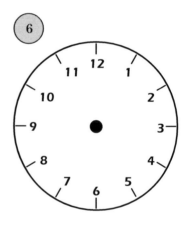

| 9:45 |

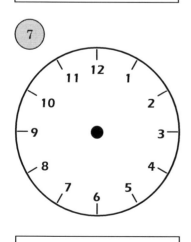

| 10:45 |

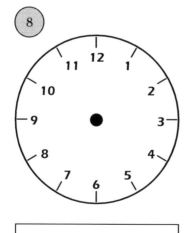

| 1:45 |

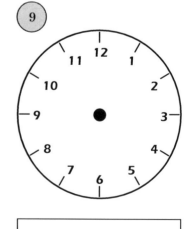

| 12:45 |

Date: _____ Start: _____ Finish: _____ Score: _____

Draw the hands to show the time.

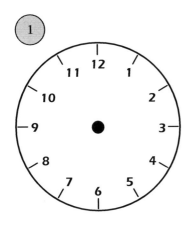

11:15

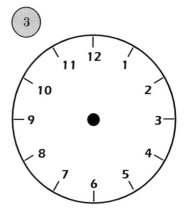

6:45

2:15

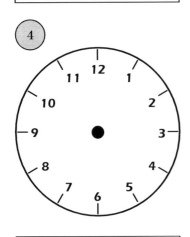

12:15

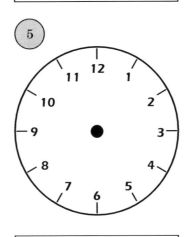

5:15

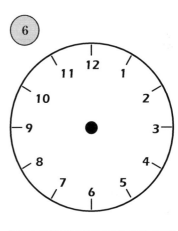

4:15

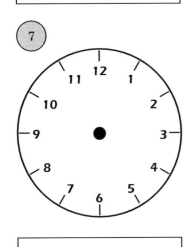

9:15

7:15

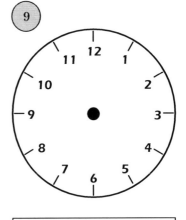

1:15

Date: _____   Start: _____   Finish: _____   Score: _____

Draw the hands to show the time.

1

4:15

2

1:45

3

7:15

4

5:15

5

11:15

6

6:15

7

3:15

8

8:15

9

12:15

Date: _____ Start: _____ Finish: _____ Score: _____

What time does the clock show? Write in the box.

1

2

3

4

5

6

7

8

9

Date: _____   Start: _____   Finish: _____   Score: _____

What time does the clock show? Write in the box.

①

②

③

④

⑤

⑥

⑦

⑧

⑨

Date:_____ Start:_____ Finish:_____ Score:_____

What time does the clock show? Write in the box.

①

②

③

④

⑤

⑥

⑦

⑧

⑨

Date: _____   Start: _____   Finish: _____   Score: _____

What time does the clock show? Write in the box.

①

②

③

④

⑤

⑥

⑦

⑧

⑨

Date:_____ Start:_____ Finish:_____ Score:_____

Draw the hands to show the time.

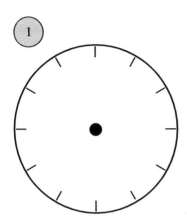

6:15

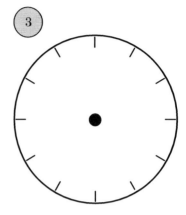

10:45

3:15

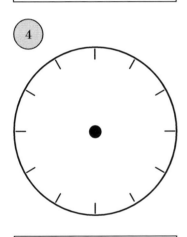

5:15

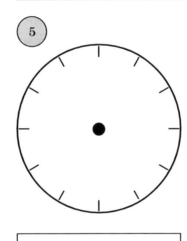

7:15

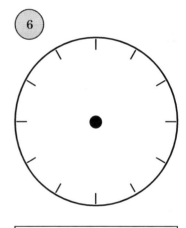

9:15

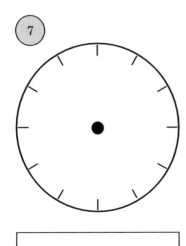

1:15

8:15

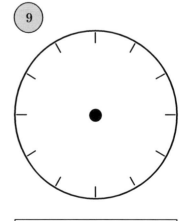

12:15

Date:_____   Start:_____   Finish:_____   Score:_____

Draw the hands to show the time.

1

5:45

2

10:15

3

2:45

4

12:45

5

6:45

6

7:45

7

3:45

8

8:45

9

9:45

Date: _____ Start: _____ Finish: _____ Score: _____

Draw the hands to show the time.

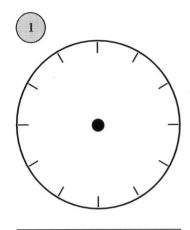

9:15

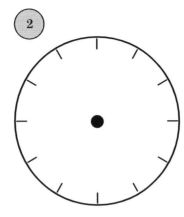

4:45

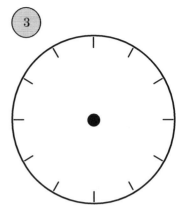

8:15

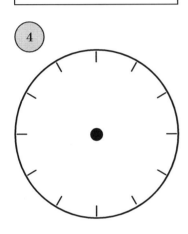

12:15

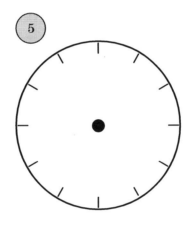

1:15

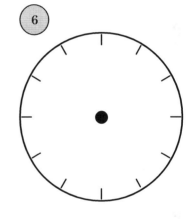

2:15

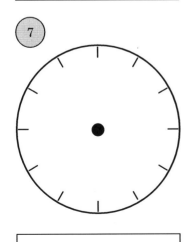

11:15

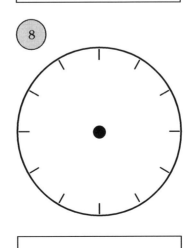

3:15

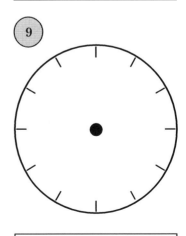

7:15

Date: _____ Start: _____ Finish: _____ Score: _____

Draw the hands to show the time.

1

3:15

2

6:45

3

12:15

4

2:15

5

7:15

6

5:15

7

9:15

8

4:15

9

11:15

Date: _____   Start: _____   Finish: _____   Score: _____

Match the analog and digital clocks that show the same time.

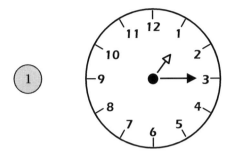
(1)

(A)
11:45

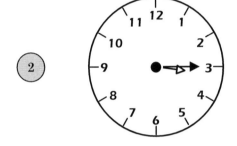
(2)

(B)
01:15

(3)

(C)
03:15

(4)

(D)
04:15

(5)

(E)
10:15

Date: _____   Start: _____   Finish: _____   Score: _____

Match the analog and digital clocks that show the same time.

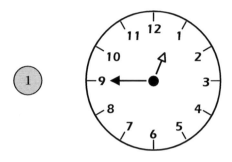

(1)

(A)
06:45

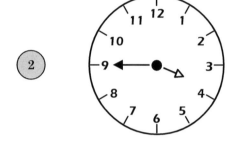

(2)

(B)
03:45

(3)

(C)
02:45

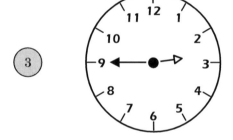

(4)

(D)
07:45

(5)

(E)
12:45

Date: _____ Start: _____ Finish: _____ Score: _____

Match the analog and digital clocks that show the same time.

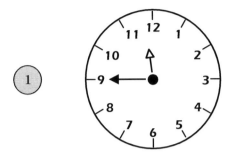

(1)

(A)  02:45

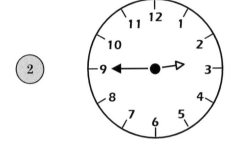

(2)

(B)  08:45

(3)

(C)  06:45

(4)

(D) 12:45

(5)

(E) 11:45

Date: _____   Start: _____   Finish: _____   Score: _____

Match the analog and digital clocks that show the same time.

(1) 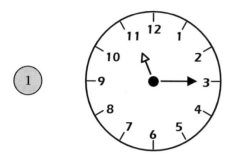   (A)

(2) 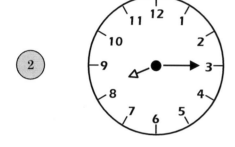   (B)

(3)    (C)

(4)    (D) 07:15

(5)   (E) 12:15

Date: _____   Start: _____   Finish: _____   Score: _____

Match the analog and digital clocks that show the same time.

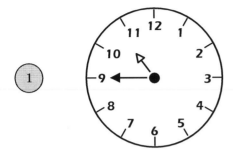   

   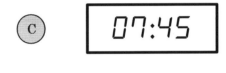

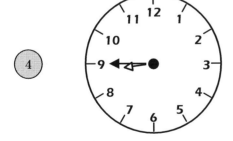

Date: _____   Start: _____   Finish: _____   Score: _____

Match the analog and digital clocks that show the same time.

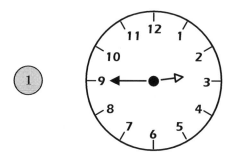

(1)

(A) `03:45`

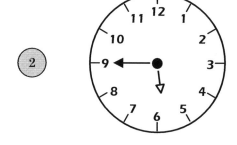

(2)

(B) `02:45`

(3)

(C) `09:45`

(4)

(D) `05:45`

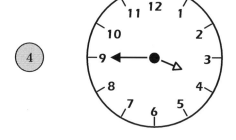

(5)

(E) `11:45`

Date: _____ Start: _____ Finish: _____ Score: _____

Write the time elapsed between two clocks.

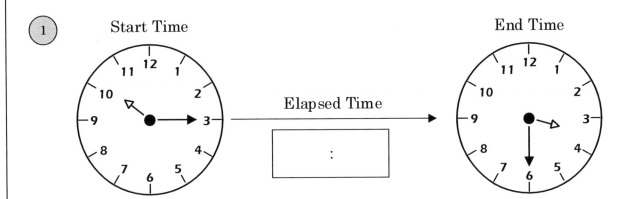

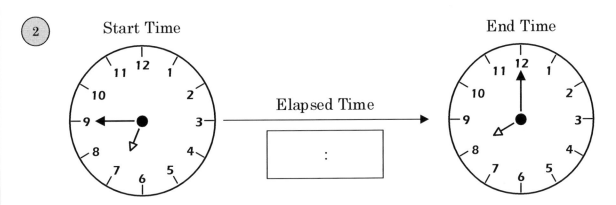

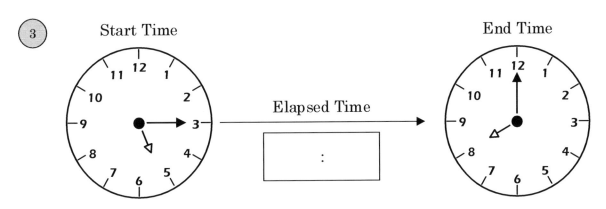

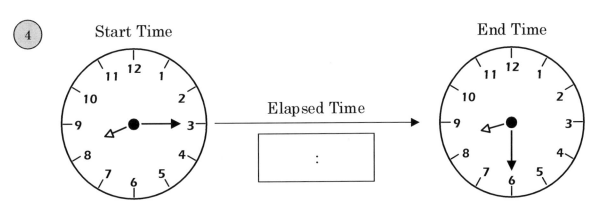

Date:_____ Start:_____ Finish:_____ Score:_____

Write the time elapsed between two clocks.

(1) Start Time

Elapsed Time

:

End Time

(2) Start Time

Elapsed Time

:

End Time

(3) Start Time

Elapsed Time

:

End Time

(4) Start Time

Elapsed Time

:

End Time

Date: _____ Start: _____ Finish: _____ Score: _____

Write the time elapsed between two clocks.

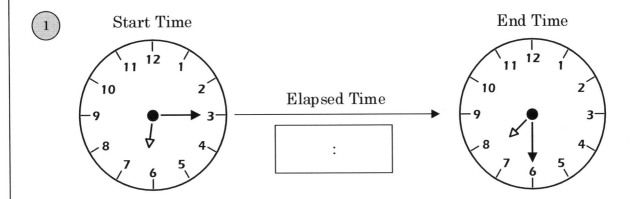

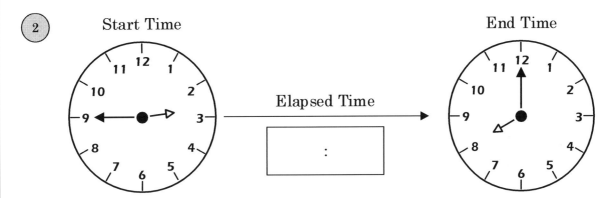

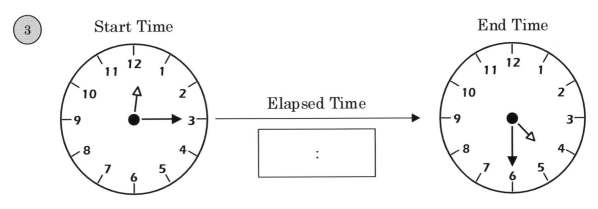

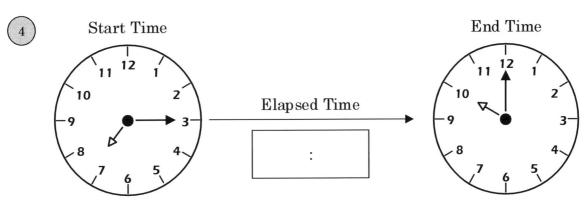

Date: _____ Start: _____ Finish: _____ Score: _____

Write the time elapsed between two clocks.

1 Start Time | Elapsed Time | End Time

Elapsed Time

[:]

2 Start Time | Elapsed Time | End Time

Elapsed Time

[:]

3 Start Time | Elapsed Time | End Time

Elapsed Time

[:]

4 Start Time | Elapsed Time | End Time

Elapsed Time

[:]

Time Telling – Introducing Quarters and Five Minutes

Date: _____ Start: _____ Finish: _____ Score: _____

Write the time elapsed between two clocks.

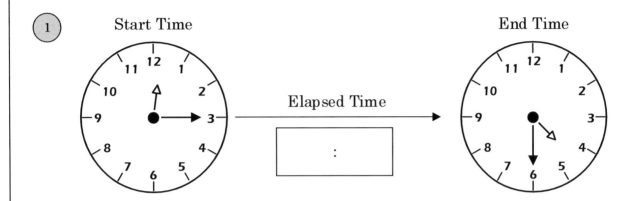

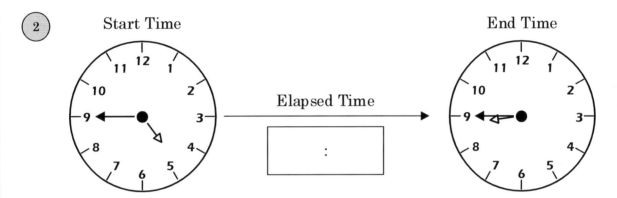

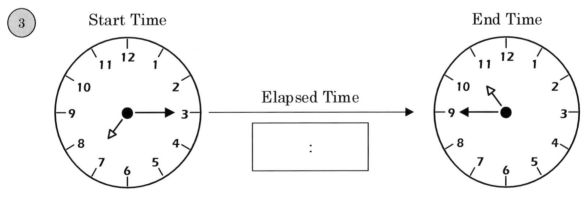

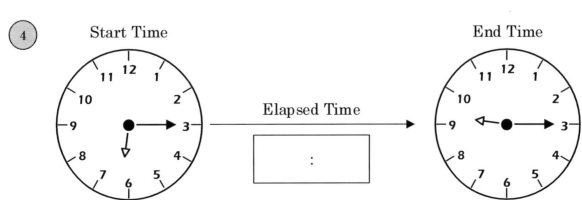

Date:_____ Start:_____ Finish:_____ Score:_____

Write the time elapsed between two clocks.

① Start Time   End Time

Elapsed Time

[:   ]

② Start Time   End Time

Elapsed Time

[:   ]

③ Start Time   End Time

Elapsed Time

[:   ]

④ Start Time   End Time

Elapsed Time

[:   ]

Date: _____ Start: _____ Finish: _____ Score: _____

Draw the hands to show the end time.

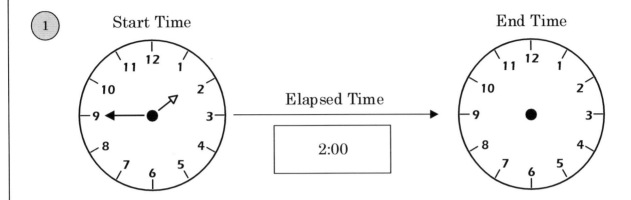

Start Time — Elapsed Time 2:00 — End Time

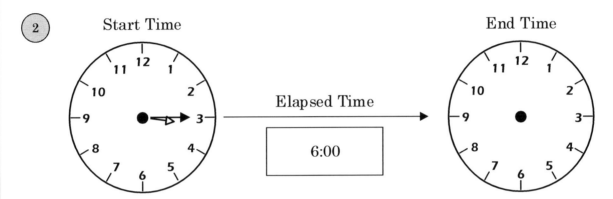

Start Time — Elapsed Time 6:00 — End Time

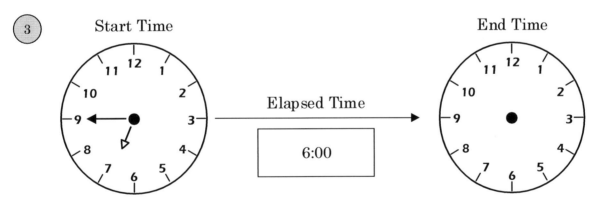

Start Time — Elapsed Time 6:00 — End Time

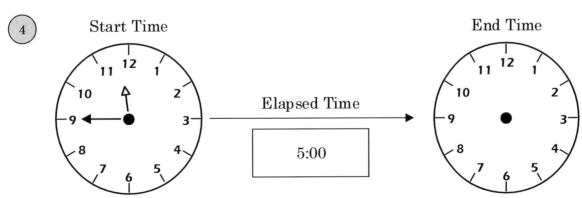

Start Time — Elapsed Time 5:00 — End Time

Draw Hands : To the Quarter Hour - Elapsed Time

Date: _____ Start: _____ Finish: _____ Score: _____

Draw the hands to show the end time.

1 Start Time   End Time

Elapsed Time

5:00

2 Start Time   End Time

Elapsed Time

3:00

3 Start Time   End Time

Elapsed Time

3:00

4 Start Time   End Time

Elapsed Time

4:00

Date: _____ Start: _____ Finish: _____ Score: _____

Draw the hands to show the end time.

1 Start Time   End Time

Elapsed Time

5:00

2 Start Time   End Time

Elapsed Time

5:00

3 Start Time   End Time

Elapsed Time

5:00

4 Start Time   End Time

Elapsed Time

5:00

Date: _____ Start: _____ Finish: _____ Score: _____

Draw the hands to show the end time.

① Start Time   End Time

Elapsed Time

6:00

② Start Time   End Time

Elapsed Time

5:00

③ Start Time   End Time

Elapsed Time

3:00

④ Start Time   End Time

Elapsed Time

3:00

Date: _____ Start: _____ Finish: _____ Score: _____

Draw the hands to show the start time.

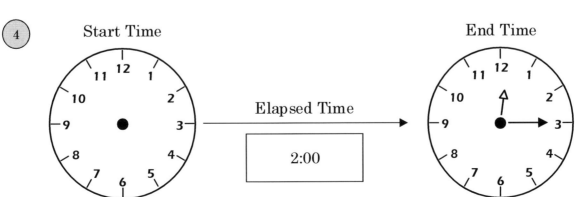

1   Start Time   End Time

Elapsed Time

4:00

2   Start Time   End Time

Elapsed Time

2:00

3   Start Time   End Time

Elapsed Time

5:00

4   Start Time   End Time

Elapsed Time

2:00

Date: _____   Start: _____   Finish: _____   Score: _____

Draw the hands to show the start time.

① Start Time   End Time
Elapsed Time
3:00

② Start Time   End Time
Elapsed Time
4:00

③ Start Time   End Time
Elapsed Time
3:00

④ Start Time   End Time
Elapsed Time
3:00

Date:_____ Start:_____ Finish:_____ Score:_____

Draw the hands to show the start time.

① Start Time   End Time

Elapsed Time

2:00

② Start Time   End Time

Elapsed Time

6:00

③ Start Time   End Time

Elapsed Time

5:00

④ Start Time   End Time

Elapsed Time

2:00

Date: _____ Start: _____ Finish: _____ Score: _____

Draw the hands to show the start time.

1   Start Time   End Time

Elapsed Time

3:00

2   Start Time   End Time

Elapsed Time

1:00

3   Start Time   End Time

Elapsed Time

3:00

4   Start Time   End Time

Elapsed Time

5:00

Date: _____ Start: _____ Finish: _____ Score: _____

Circle the clock indicating the correct time.

① Hanna decided to take a science class. The class started at 12:00 PM and lasted for an hour and 45 minutes. What time did the class end?

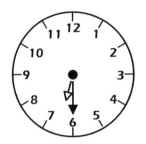 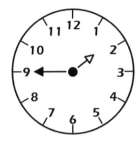 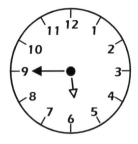 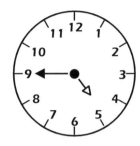

② It takes an hour and 45 minutes for Selena's dad to repair a broken truck. He finished repairing at 02:30 PM. What time he started?

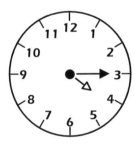 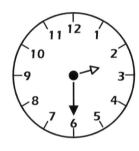 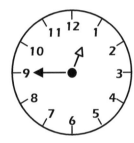 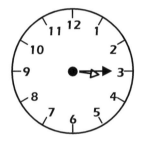

③ Kira left school at 03:00 PM. It takes her an hour to reach home. When will she get home?

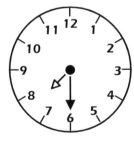 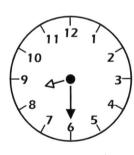 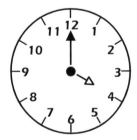 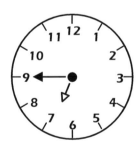

④ Jessica and Emma just finished watching a movie for 3 hours. If they started watching the movie at 06:30 PM what time the clock shows now?

 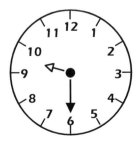 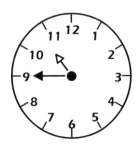 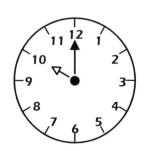

Date: _____ Start: _____ Finish: _____ Score: _____

Circle the clock indicating the correct time.

1. Isabel started for library along with her brother Samuel at 12:00 PM. It took her an hour and 45 minutes in the line to return books. What time did they return the books?

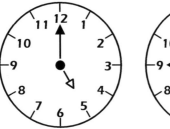 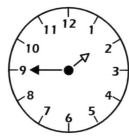  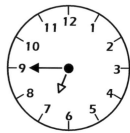

2. Alejandro arrived at a restaurant for dinner at 06:45 PM. He placed his order, ate, and paid the bill. He left the restaurant 2 hours later. What time was it when Alejandro left the restaurant?

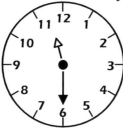  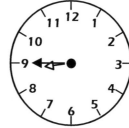 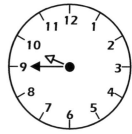

3. Corey and Nadia talked on the phone for an hour. What time were they done talking on the phone if Corey called Nadia at 06:15 PM?

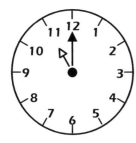 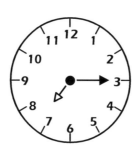 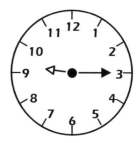 

4. The class was given an hour and 15 minutes to complete the assignment. What time will the assignment need to be completed if the teacher handed out the assignment at 12:00 PM?

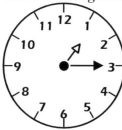  

Date: _____ Start: _____ Finish: _____ Score: _____

Circle the clock indicating the correct time.

1 Marcus was preparing for a report presentation at his school. His old printer takes 30 minutes to print a report. If he was done printing at 03:30 PM, what time did he start printing the report?

 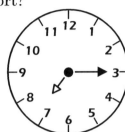 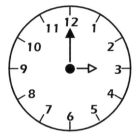

2 Camryn and Elena just finished watching a movie for 2 hours and 45 minutes. If they started watching the movie at 06:30 PM what time the clock shows now?

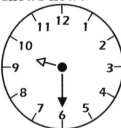 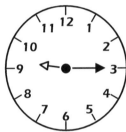  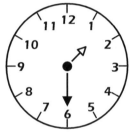

3 Eli arrived at a restaurant for dinner at 05:45 PM. He placed his order, ate, and paid the bill. He left the restaurant an hour later. What time was it when Eli left the restaurant?

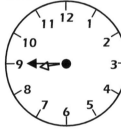   

4 Aliyah decided to write a letter to her grandfather. After spending 30 minutes she could finish writing at 05:45 PM. What time was it when Aliyah started writing the letter?

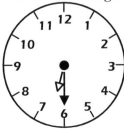 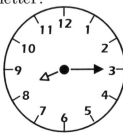 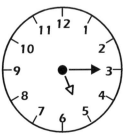

Date: _____   Start: _____   Finish: _____   Score: _____

Circle the clock indicating the correct time.

1 It was 02:45 PM when Ruby began cleaning the yard. It took her 3 hours to clean all the leaves into piles and stuffed them into bags. When did Ruby finish cleaning the yard?

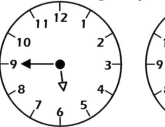 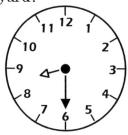 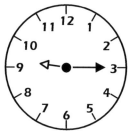 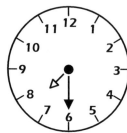

2 Gage and Briana talked on the phone for an hour. What time were they done talking on the phone if Gage called Briana at 06:15 PM?

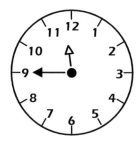 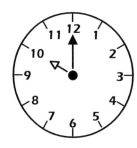 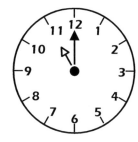 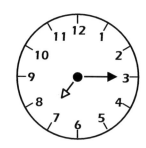

3 It took Briana an hour to walk to the school. What time did Briana arrive at the school if she started at 09:15 AM?

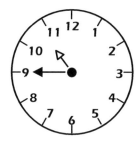 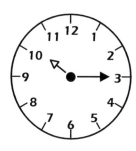 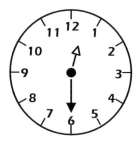 

4 Stella played a game on her iPad for an hour and 15 minutes. If she started playing at 05:15 PM, what time did Stella stop playing?

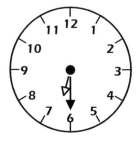 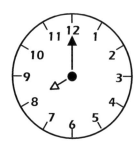 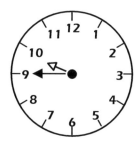 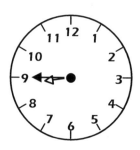

Date: _____   Start: _____   Finish: _____   Score: _____

Circle the clock indicating the correct time.

① Jaylen was preparing for a report presentation at his school. His old printer takes 30 minutes to print a report. If he was done printing at 03:45 PM, what time did he start printing the report?

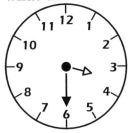 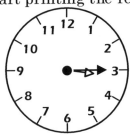 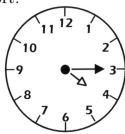 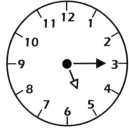

② Paris called Katie at 07:00 PM. If they talked for 45 minutes, what time were they finished talking?

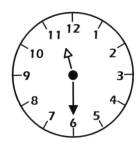 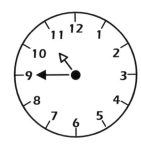 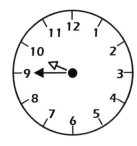 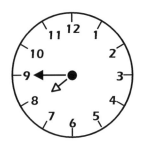

③ It was 11:45 AM when Natalie began cleaning the yard. It took her 2 hours and 15 minutes to clean all the leaves into piles and stuffed them into bags. When did Natalie finish cleaning the yard?

④ It takes an hour and 15 minutes for Clara's dad to repair a broken truck. He finished repairing at 01:30 PM. What time he started?

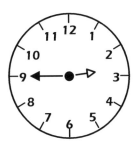 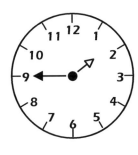 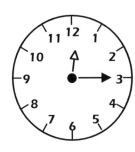 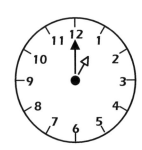

Date: _____   Start: _____   Finish: _____   Score: _____

Circle the clock indicating the correct time.

1 Arianna left school at 03:15 PM. It takes her an hour to reach home. When will she get home?

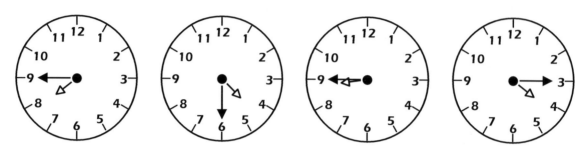

2 Mariana was going on a vacation to Florida. Her flight is scheduled to depart at 11:45 AM and is expected to take 4 hours to reach Orlando. What time the plane is scheduled to land?

3 Gracie started for library along with her brother Connor at 11:00 AM. It took her an hour and 30 minutes in the line to return books. What time did they return the books?

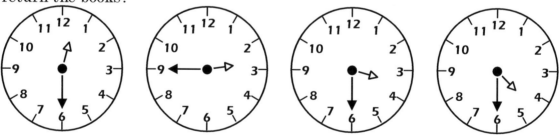

4 Alexandria called Kelsey at 09:00 PM. If they talked for an hour, what time were they finished talking?

Date:_____ Start:_____ Finish:_____ Score:_____

Draw the missing hands as per the time pattern.

Date: _____   Start: _____   Finish: _____   Score: _____

Draw the missing hands as per the time pattern.

Date: _____ Start: _____ Finish: _____ Score: _____

Draw the missing hands as per the time pattern.

Date: _____   Start: _____   Finish: _____   Score: _____

Draw the missing hands as per the time pattern.

Time Telling – Introducing Quarters and Five Minutes

Date: _____ Start: _____ Finish: _____ Score: _____

What time does the clock show? Fill the box. Example: Twenty Five past two.

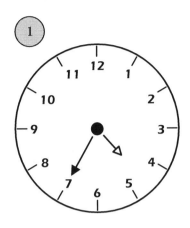

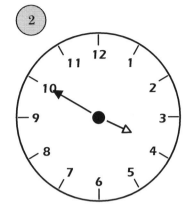

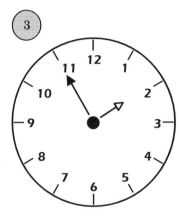

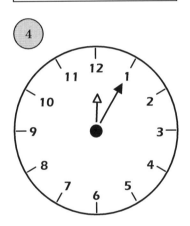

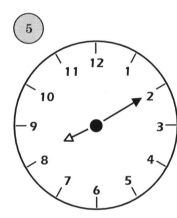

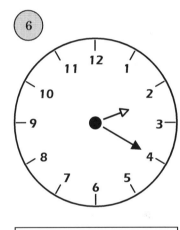

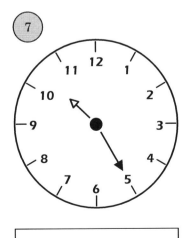

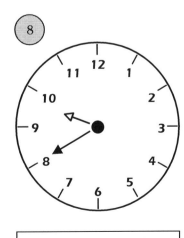

Date: _____   Start: _____   Finish: _____   Score: _____

What time does the clock show? Fill the box. Example: Twenty Five past two.

(1)

(2)

(3)

(4)

(5)

(6)

(7)

(8)

(9)

Time Telling – Introducing Quarters and Five Minutes

Date: _____ Start: _____ Finish: _____ Score: _____

What time does the clock show? Fill the box. Example: Twenty Five past two.

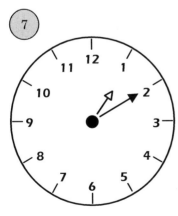

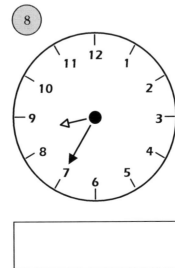

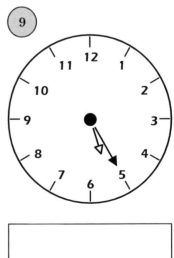

Read Time : To The Five Minutes - In Words

Date:____________ Start:____________ Finish:____________ Score:____________

What time does the clock show? Fill the box. Example: Twenty Five past two.

1

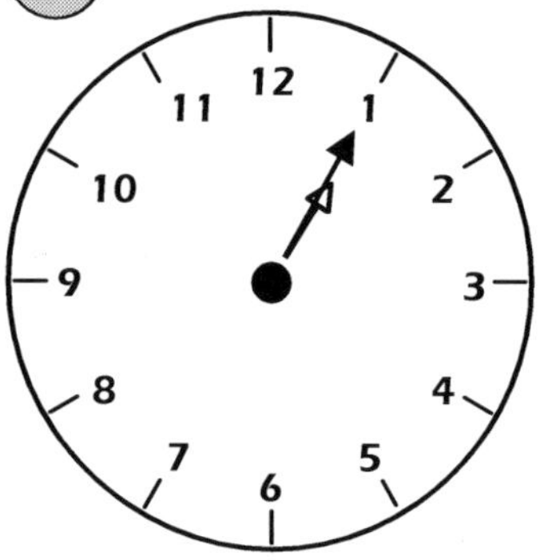

2

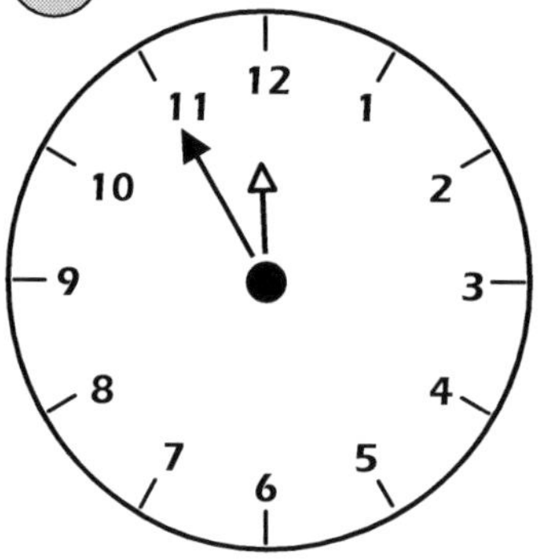

3

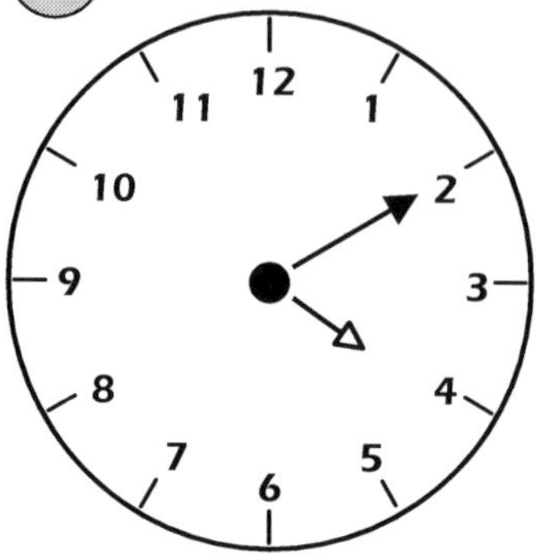

4

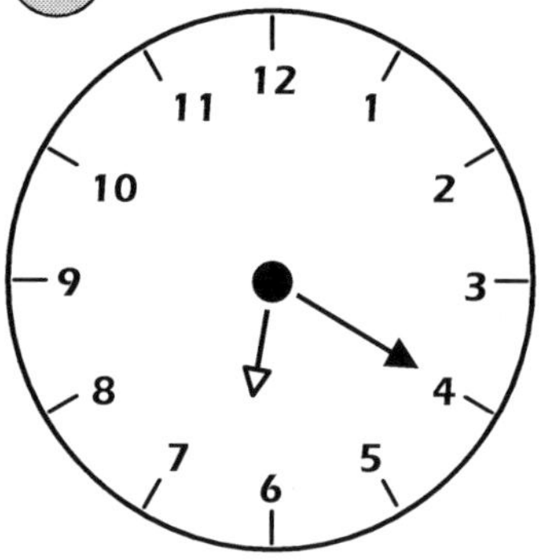

5

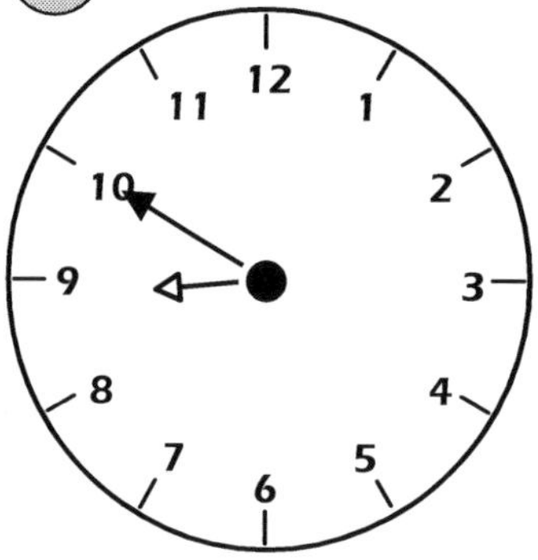

6

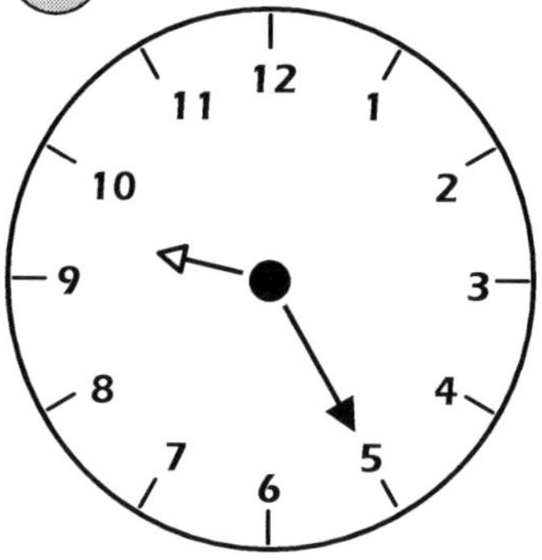

7

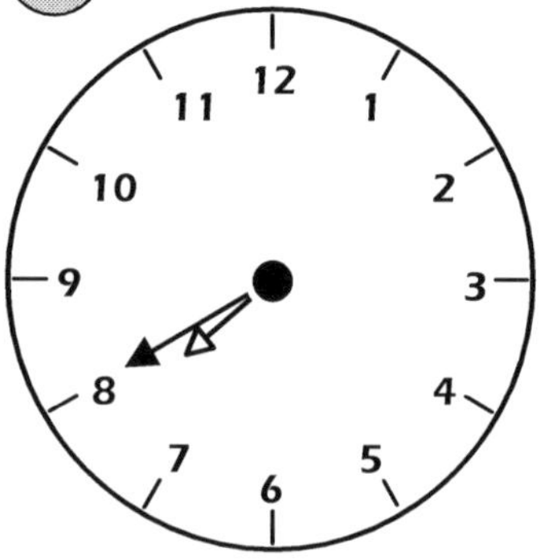

8

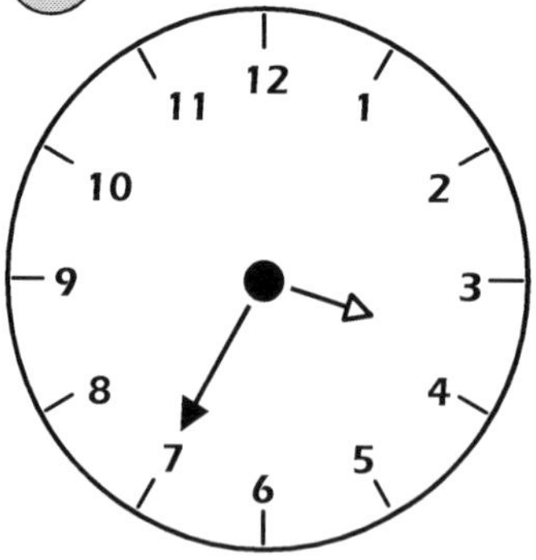

9

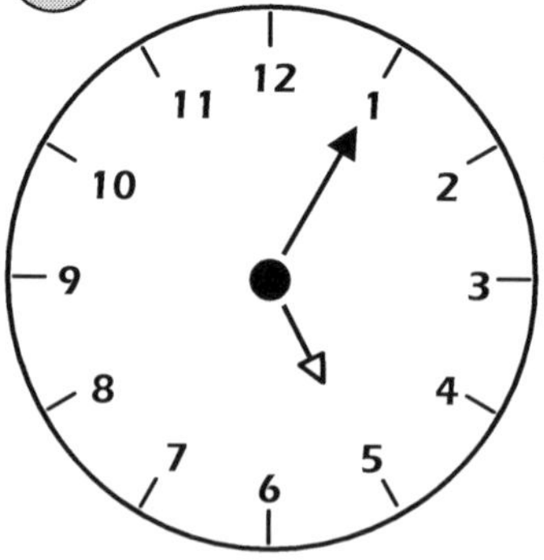

Date: _____ Start: _____ Finish: _____ Score: _____

Draw the hands to show the time.

①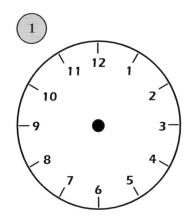

Twenty to twelve

②

Ten to eleven

③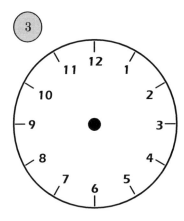

Twenty past nine

④

Twenty Five to two

⑤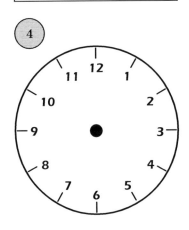

Ten past seven

⑥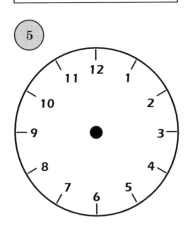

Five past eight

⑦

Twenty Five past four

⑧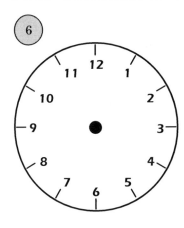

Five to four

⑨

Twenty to seven

Date: _____ Start: _____ Finish: _____ Score: _____

Draw the hands to show the time.

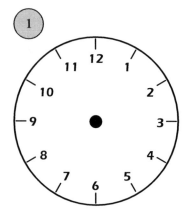

Ten past two

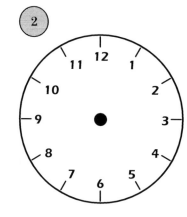

Five past five

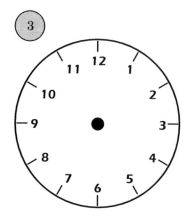

Twenty past twelve

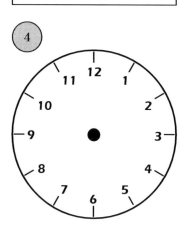

Twenty Five to ten

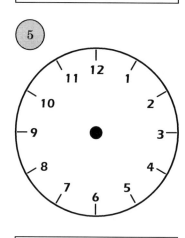

Twenty to eight

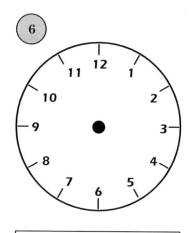

Ten to twelve

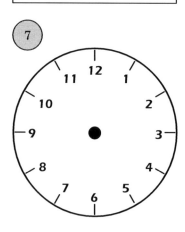

Five to five

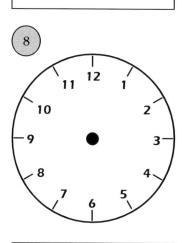

Twenty Five past ten

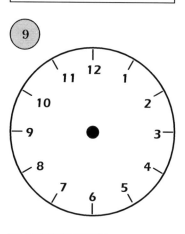

Ten past three

Date: _____ Start: _____ Finish: _____ Score: _____

What time does the clock show? Write in the box. Example: 2:35.

(1)

(2)

(3)

(4)

(5)

(6)

(7)

(8)

(9)

Date: _____ Start: _____ Finish: _____ Score: _____

What time does the clock show? Write in the box. Example: 2:35.

①

②

③

④

⑤

⑥

⑦

⑧

⑨

Time Telling – Introducing Quarters and Five Minutes

Date: _____ Start: _____ Finish: _____ Score: _____

What time does the clock show? Write in the box. Example: 2:35.

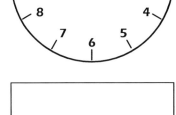
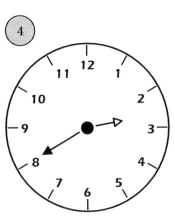
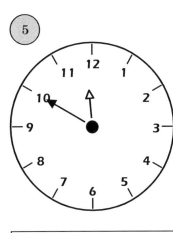
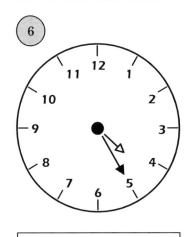

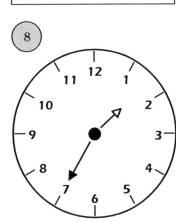
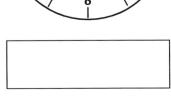

Time Telling – Introducing Quarters and Five Minutes

77

Date: _____   Start: _____   Finish: _____   Score: _____

What time does the clock show? Write in the box. Example: 2:35.

Time Telling – Introducing Quarters and Five Minutes

Date: _____ Start: _____ Finish: _____ Score: _____

Draw the hands to show the time.

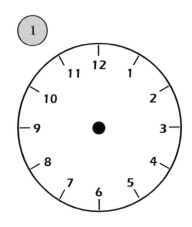

12:40

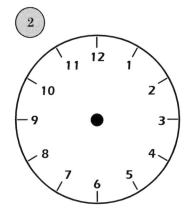

11:55

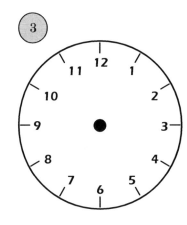

2:50

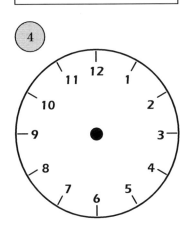

5:05

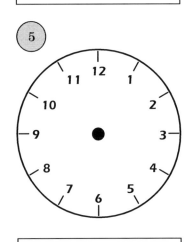

8:10

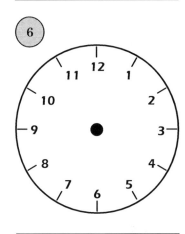

10:20

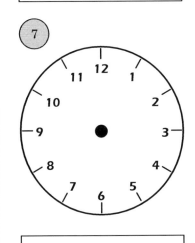

9:25

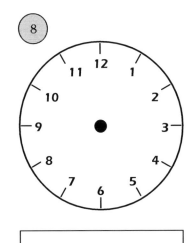

1:35

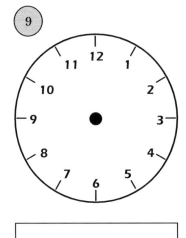

6:40

Date: _____ Start: _____ Finish: _____ Score: _____

Draw the hands to show the time.

① 6:50

② 7:25

③ 12:10

④ 10:35

⑤ 5:05

⑥ 11:20

⑦ 9:55

⑧ 2:40

⑨ 4:50

Time Telling – Introducing Quarters and Five Minutes

Date:_____ Start:_____ Finish:_____ Score:_____

What time does the clock show? Write in the box.

①

②

③

④

⑤

⑥

⑦

⑧

⑨

Date: _____   Start: _____   Finish: _____   Score: _____

What time does the clock show? Write in the box.

1

2

3

4

5

6

7

8

9

Date:_____ Start:_____ Finish:_____ Score:_____

Draw the hands to show the time.

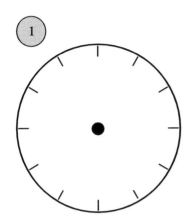

12:20

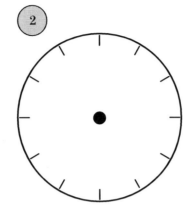

8:10

6:55

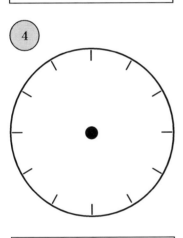

5:50

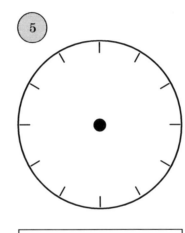

9:05

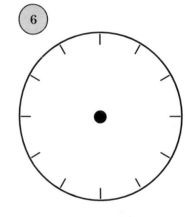

2:35

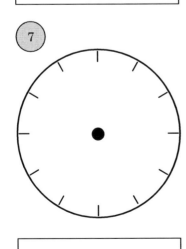

10:40

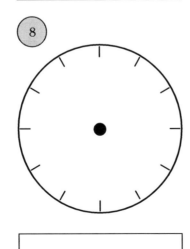

4:25

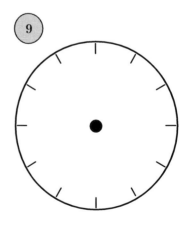

11:20

Date:_____ Start:_____ Finish:_____ Score:_____

Draw the hands to show the time.

①

2:55

②

6:25

③

4:50

④

1:20

⑤

7:10

⑥

9:40

⑦

11:35

⑧

10:05

⑨

5:55

Date: _____ Start: _____ Finish: _____ Score: _____

Match the analog and digital clocks that show the same time.

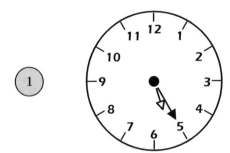

(1)

(A)

(2)

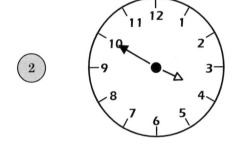

(B)

(3)

(C)

(4)

(D)

(5)

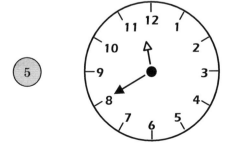

(E) 09:35

Date: _____   Start: _____   Finish: _____   Score: _____

Match the analog and digital clocks that show the same time.

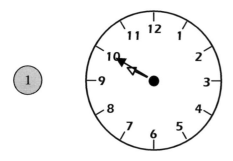 

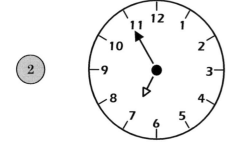 

Date: _____ Start: _____ Finish: _____ Score: _____

Write the time elapsed between two clocks.

(1) Start Time

End Time

Elapsed Time

[:]

(2) Start Time

End Time

Elapsed Time

[:]

(3) Start Time

End Time

Elapsed Time

[:]

(4) Start Time

End Time

Elapsed Time

[:]

Date: _____ Start: _____ Finish: _____ Score: _____

Write the time elapsed between two clocks.

1

Start Time

End Time

Elapsed Time

☐ : ☐

2

Start Time

End Time

Elapsed Time

☐ : ☐

3

Start Time

End Time

Elapsed Time

☐ : ☐

4

Start Time

End Time

Elapsed Time

☐ : ☐

Time Telling – Introducing Quarters and Five Minutes

Date: _____ Start: _____ Finish: _____ Score: _____

Write the time elapsed between two clocks.

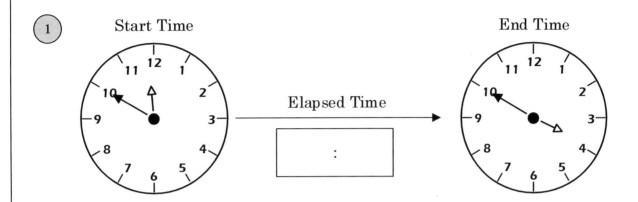

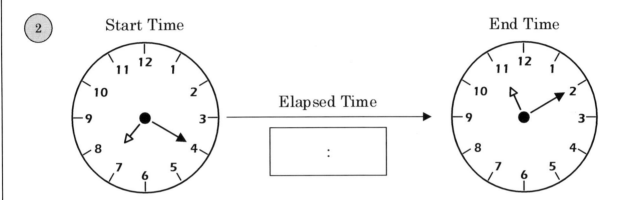

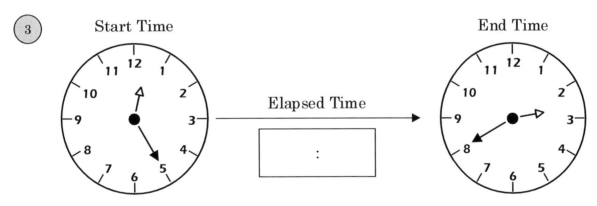

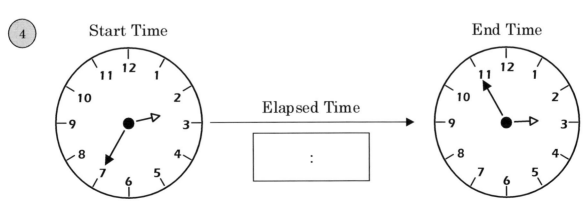

Date:_____ Start:_____ Finish:_____ Score:_____

Write the time elapsed between two clocks.

1   Start Time   End Time

Elapsed Time

[:   ]

2   Start Time   End Time

Elapsed Time

[:   ]

3   Start Time   End Time

Elapsed Time

[:   ]

4   Start Time   End Time

Elapsed Time

[:   ]

Date: _____   Start: _____   Finish: _____   Score: _____

Draw the hands to show the end time.

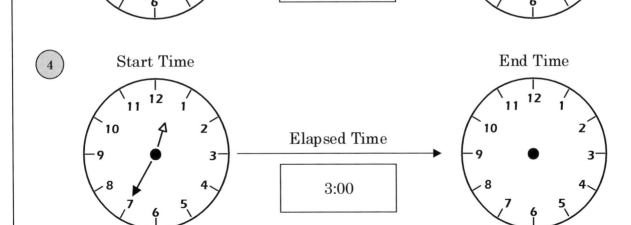

1   Start Time   End Time

    Elapsed Time

    4:00

2   Start Time   End Time

    Elapsed Time

    2:00

3   Start Time   End Time

    Elapsed Time

    3:00

4   Start Time   End Time

    Elapsed Time

    3:00

Date: _____ Start: _____ Finish: _____ Score: _____

Draw the hands to show the end time.

1   Start Time   End Time

Elapsed Time

5:00

2   Start Time   End Time

Elapsed Time

2:00

3   Start Time   End Time

Elapsed Time

2:00

4   Start Time   End Time

Elapsed Time

2:00

Date:_____ Start:_____ Finish:_____ Score:_____

Draw the hands to show the start time.

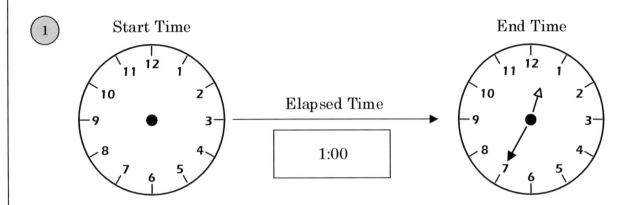

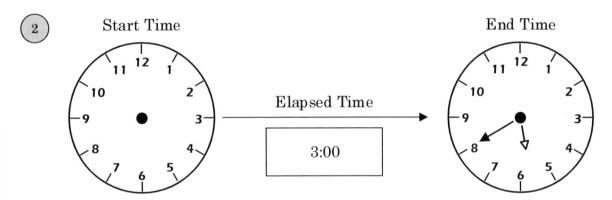

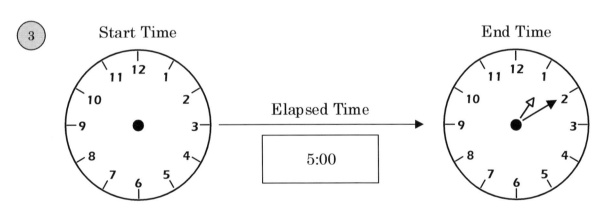

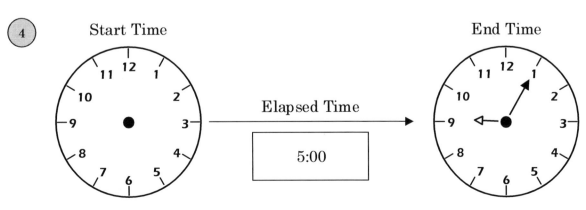

Date: _____   Start: _____   Finish: _____   Score: _____

Draw the hands to show the start time.

1   Start Time   Elapsed Time   End Time

        3:00

2   Start Time   Elapsed Time   End Time

        1:00

3   Start Time   Elapsed Time   End Time

        6:00

4   Start Time   Elapsed Time   End Time

        2:00

Date: _____   Start: _____   Finish: _____   Score: _____

Circle the clock indicating the correct time.

① Henry goes for a an hour and 20 minutes bike ride every day. Today, he begins his ride at 08:05 AM. What time will Henry finish riding his bike?

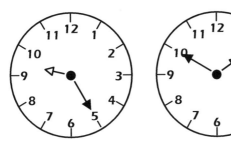 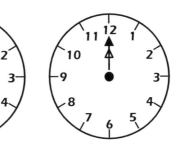 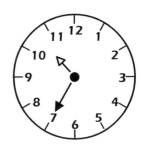

② Eduardo was preparing for a report presentation at his school. His old printer takes 35 minutes to print a report. If he was done printing at 03:45 PM, what time did he start printing the report?

  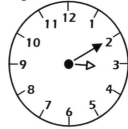 

③ Maria's favorite TV show is on at 02:40 PM and she still has 2 hours and 30 minutes until the show will be on. What is the current time?

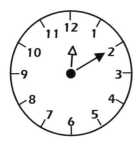 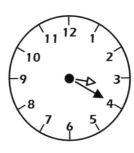 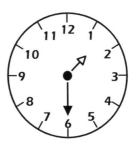 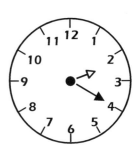

④ Savannah started for library along with her brother Christopher at 11:10 AM. It took her an hour and 30 minutes in the line to return books. What time did they return the books?

Date: _____ Start: _____ Finish: _____ Score: _____

Circle the clock indicating the correct time.

① Haley and Mariana just finished watching a movie for 2 hours and 25 minutes. If they started watching the movie at 05:20 PM what time the clock shows now?

 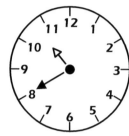 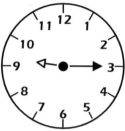 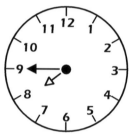

② Alexandria played a game on her iPad for an hour. If she started playing at 04:30 PM, what time did Alexandria stop playing?

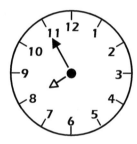 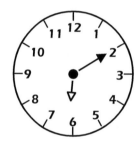 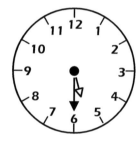 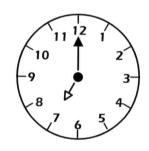

③ Clayton goes for a an hour and 15 minutes bike ride every day. Today, he begins his ride at 07:55 AM. What time will Clayton finish riding his bike?

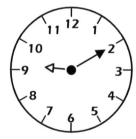 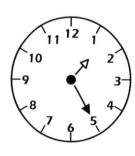 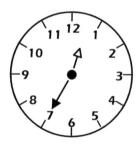 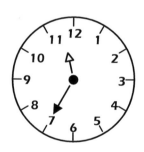

④ Cynthia just came home from a grocery store and clock shows 06:25 PM. If it took her 35 minutes to reach home from the store, what time did she leave the store?

 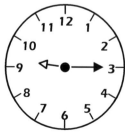  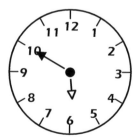

Time Telling – Introducing Quarters and Five Minutes

Date: _____   Start: _____   Finish: _____   Score: _____

Draw the missing hands as per the time pattern.

Date: _____   Start: _____   Finish: _____   Score: _____

Draw the missing hands as per the time pattern.

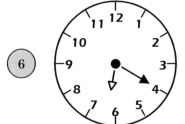

Answer Key

Answer Key

Page 7

1. Quarter to seven
2. Quarter past eleven
3. Quarter to eleven
4. Quarter to three
5. Quarter to four
6. Quarter to two
7. Quarter to ten
8. Quarter to nine
9. Quarter to eight

Page 8

1. Quarter to eight
2. Quarter past two
3. Quarter to thirteen
4. Quarter to ten
5. Quarter to two
6. Quarter to five
7. Quarter to twelve
8. Quarter to seven
9. Quarter to eleven

Page 9

1. Quarter past twelve
2. Quarter to six
3. Quarter past six
4. Quarter past eight
5. Quarter past seven
6. Quarter past ten
7. Quarter past four
8. Quarter past one
9. Quarter past eleven

Page 10

1. Quarter to twelve
2. Quarter past two
3. Quarter to eight

4. Quarter to thirteen
5. Quarter to four
6. Quarter to five
7. Quarter to six
8. Quarter to ten
9. Quarter to nine

Page 11

1. Quarter past seven
2. Quarter to nine
3. Quarter past four
4. Quarter past three
5. Quarter past one
6. Quarter past nine
7. Quarter past two
8. Quarter past twelve
9. Quarter past eleven

Page 12

1. Quarter to seven
2. Quarter past twelve
3. Quarter to eleven
4. Quarter to ten
5. Quarter to eight
6. Quarter to nine
7. Quarter to five
8. Quarter to six
9. Quarter to three

Page 13

1.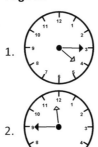

2.

3.

4.

5.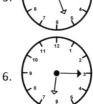

6.

7.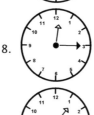

8.

9.

Page 14

1.

2.

3.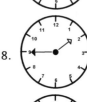

4.

5.

7.

8.

3.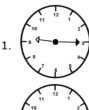

5.

6.

8.

9.

Page 15

1.

2.

3.

4.

5.

6.

Time Telling – Introducing Quarters and Five Minutes

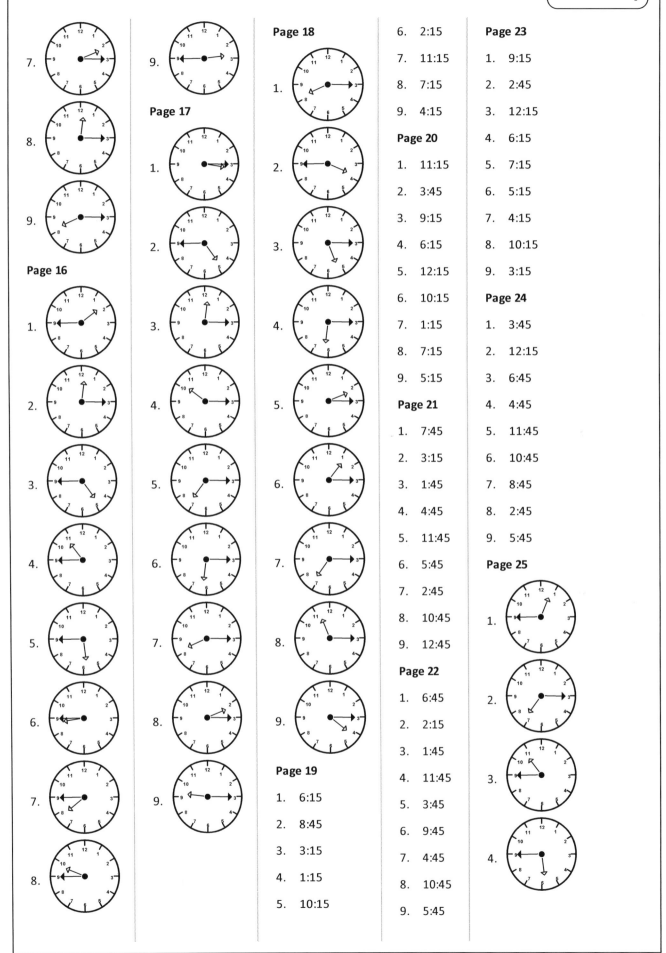

7.

8.

9.

Page 16

1.

2.

3.

4.

5.

6.

7.

8.

9.

Page 17

1.

2.

3.

4.

5.

6.

7.

8.

9.

Page 18

1.

2.

3.

4.

5.

6.

7.

8.

9.

Page 19

1. 6:15
2. 8:45
3. 3:15
4. 1:15
5. 10:15
6. 2:15
7. 11:15
8. 7:15
9. 4:15

Page 20

1. 11:15
2. 3:45
3. 9:15
4. 6:15
5. 12:15
6. 10:15
7. 1:15
8. 7:15
9. 5:15

Page 21

1. 7:45
2. 3:15
3. 1:45
4. 4:45
5. 11:45
6. 5:45
7. 2:45
8. 10:45
9. 12:45

Page 22

1. 6:45
2. 2:15
3. 1:45
4. 11:45
5. 3:45
6. 9:45
7. 4:45
8. 10:45
9. 5:45

Page 23

1. 9:15
2. 2:45
3. 12:15
4. 6:15
5. 7:15
6. 5:15
7. 4:15
8. 10:15
9. 3:15

Page 24

1. 3:45
2. 12:15
3. 6:45
4. 4:45
5. 11:45
6. 10:45
7. 8:45
8. 2:45
9. 5:45

Page 25

1.

2.

3.

4.

Page 29

Page 28

Page 27

Page 26

Page 30

Page 31

1. 7:45
2. 1:15
3. 4:45
4. 2:45
5. 9:45
6. 12:45
7. 5:45
8. 11:45
9. 6:45

Page 32

1. 12:45
2. 5:15
3. 6:45
4. 1:45
5. 7:45
6. 10:45
7. 11:45
8. 2:45
9. 9:45

Page 33

1. 6:45
2. 11:15
3. 9:45
4. 5:45
5. 3:45
6. 1:45
7. 2:45
8. 8:45
9. 12:45

Page 34

1. 3:45
2. 12:15
3. 4:45
4. 5:45
5. 6:45
6. 8:45
7. 7:45
8. 11:45
9. 9:45

Page 35

1.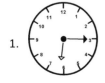

Page 36

1.
2.
3.

Page 37

1.
2.
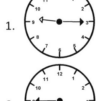

Page 38

1.
2.

Page 39

1. 1 --> B
2. 2 --> C
3. 3 --> E
4. 4 --> A
5. 5 --> D

Page 40

1. 1 --> E
2. 2 --> B
3. 3 --> C
4. 4 --> D
5. 5 --> A

Page 41

1. 1 --> E
2. 2 --> A
3. 3 --> C
4. 4 --> D
5. 5 --> B

Page 42

1. 1 --> C
2. 2 --> B
3. 3 --> D
4. 4 --> E
5. 5 --> A

Page 43

1. 1 --> B
2. 2 --> E
3. 3 --> C

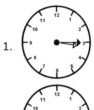

4.   4 --> A

5.   5 --> D

Page 44

1.   1 --> B

2.   2 --> D

3.   3 --> C

4.   4 --> A

5.   5 --> E

Page 45

1.   5:15

2.   1:15

3.   2:45

4.   0:15

Page 46

1.   0:15

2.   4:45

3.   0:45

4.   4:45

Page 47

1.   1:15

2.   5:15

3.   4:15

4.   2:45

Page 48

1.   2:15

2.   0:30

3.   2:30

4.   0:45

Page 49

1.   4:15

2.   4:00

3.   3:30

4.   3:00

Page 50

1.   5:15

2.   4:30

3.   1:45

4.   1:00

Page 51

1.

2.

3.

4.

Page 52

1.

2.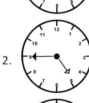

3.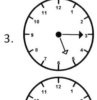

4.

Page 53

1.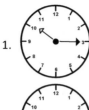

2.

3.

4.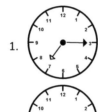

Page 54

1.

2.

3.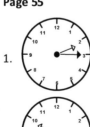

4.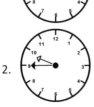

Page 55

1.

2.

Page 56

1.

2.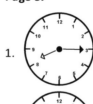

3.

4.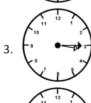

Page 57

1.

2.

3.

4.

3.

4.

Page 58

1.

2.

Page 59

1.

2.

3.

4.

Page 60

1.

2.

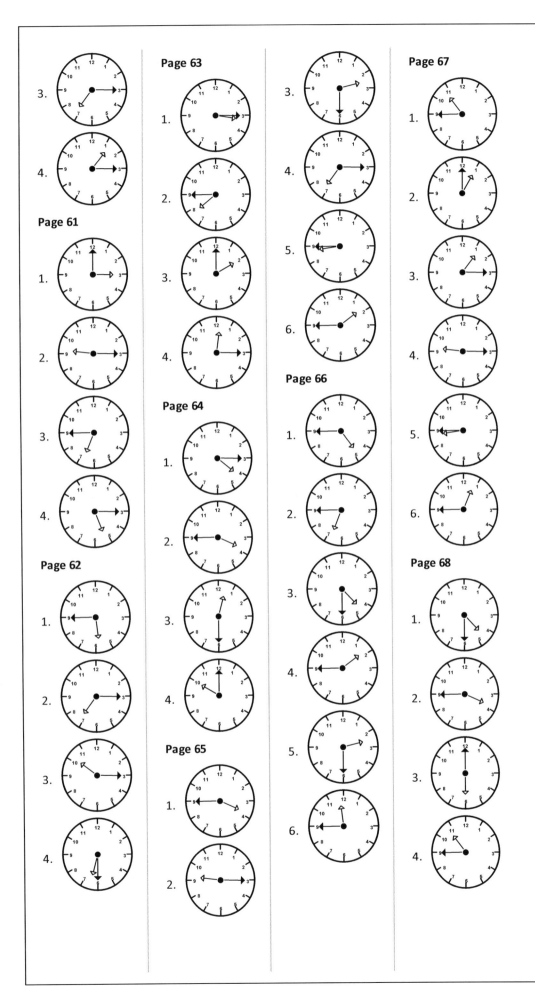

Page 63

Page 61

Page 62

Page 64

Page 65

Page 66

Page 67

Page 68

5.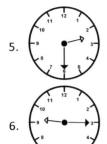

6.

Page 69

1. Twenty Five to five
2. Ten to four
3. Five to two
4. Five past twelve
5. Ten past eight
6. Twenty past two
7. Twenty Five past ten
8. Twenty to ten
9. Twenty Five to seven

Page 70

1. Five to ten
2. Twenty past three
3. Ten to eleven
4. Twenty to seven
5. Twenty Five past one
6. Twenty Five to six
7. Five past twelve
8. Ten past eleven
9. Five to five

Page 71

1. Twenty Five past two
2. Ten to eleven
3. Twenty past six
4. Five past twelve
5. Twenty to ten
6. Five to eight
7. Ten past one

8. Twenty Five to nine
9. Twenty Five past five

Page 72

1. Five past one
2. Five to twelve
3. Ten past four
4. Twenty past six
5. Ten to nine
6. Twenty Five past nine
7. Twenty to eight
8. Twenty Five to four
9. Five past five

Page 73

1.

2.

3.

4.

5.

6.

7.

8.

9.

Page 75

1. 10:20
2. 12:40
3. 4:25
4. 9:10
5. 8:55
6. 3:35
7. 2:50
8. 6:05
9. 7:20

Page 74

1.

2.

3.

4.

5.

6.

7.

8.

9.

Page 76

1. 12:10
2. 4:25
3. 6:05
4. 2:20
5. 5:35
6. 8:40
7. 9:50
8. 11:55
9. 3:10

Page 77

1. 10:55
2. 5:20
3. 8:10
4. 2:40
5. 11:50
6. 4:25
7. 9:05
8. 1:35
9. 12:55

Page 78

1. 2:50
2. 5:40
3. 8:05

4. 1:20
5. 10:25
6. 6:10
7. 9:35
8. 12:55
9. 4:50

Page 79

1.
2.
3.
4.
5.
6.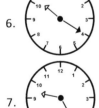
7.
8.
9.

Page 80

1.
2.
3.
4.
5.
6.
7.
8.
9.

Page 81

1. 10:50
2. 6:40
3. 9:05
4. 1:10
5. 8:55

6. 5:25
7. 12:20
8. 7:35
9. 2:50

Page 82

1. 3:40
2. 1:25
3. 7:55
4. 10:20
5. 12:10
6. 2:05
7. 8:50
8. 4:35
9. 11:40

Page 83

1.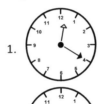
2.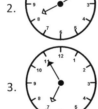
3.
4.
5.
6.

7.
8.
9.

Page 84

1.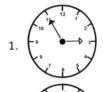
2.
3.
4.
5.
6.
7.
8.

9.

Page 85

1. 1 --> D
2. 2 --> C
3. 3 --> E
4. 4 --> A
5. 5 --> B

Page 86

1. 1 --> C
2. 2 --> E
3. 3 --> A
4. 4 --> B
5. 5 --> D

Page 87

1. 1:00
2. 5:00
3. 3:05
4. 0:10

Page 88

1. 2:00
2. 5:30
3. 1:15
4. 3:30

Page 89

1. 4:00
2. 3:50
3. 2:15
4. 0:20

Page 90

1. 5:00
2. 4:20
3. 0:25

4. 3:40

Page 91

1.

2.

3.

4.

Page 92

1.

2.

3.

4.

Page 93

1.

2.

3.

4.

Page 94

1.

2.

3.

4.

Page 95

1.

2.

3.

4.

Page 96

1.

2.

3.

4.

Page 97

1.

2.

3.

4.

5.

6.

Page 98

1.

2.

3.

4.

5.

6.

Made in the USA
Middletown, DE
09 March 2017